# Stephen Strasburg

By Jeff Savage

Lerner Publications Company • Minneapolis

Lerner Publications Company
A division of Lerner Publishing Group, Inc.
241 First Avenue North
Minneapolis, MN 55401 U.S.A.

Website address: www.lernerbooks.com


Library of Congress Cataloging-in-Publication Data

Savage, Jeff, 1961–
    Stephen Strasburg / by Jeff Savage.
      p.   cm. — (Amazing athletes)
    Includes index.
    ISBN 978–1–4677–1100–5 (lib. bdg. : alk. paper)
    1. Strasburg, Stephen, 1988-—Juvenile literature. 2. Baseball players—United States—Biography—Juvenile literature. 3. Pitchers (Baseball)—United States—Biography—Juvenile literature. I. Title.
GV865.S867S38 2013
796.357092—dc23 [B]                          2012038056

Manufactured in the United States of America
1 – BP – 12/31/12

# TABLE OF CONTENTS

Stephen Strasburg winds up for a pitch against the Atlanta Braves on August 21, 2012.

# STRIKEOUT MASTER

Stephen Strasburg threw the pitch. The baseball hissed through the air. It popped into the catcher's mitt. The **fastball** was clocked at 100 miles per hour. Stephen is the **ace** pitcher for Major League Baseball's (MLB) Washington Nationals. He stands 6 feet 4 inches tall and weighs 220 pounds. His body is packed with muscles.

Stephen was pitching in this important 2012 game against the Atlanta Braves. The Nationals were leading the Braves by six games in the **National League (NL) East**. A victory would help the Nationals make the **playoffs**. The crowd of 33,888 at Nationals Park in Washington, D.C., thought Stephen could beat the Braves. After all, he led the NL in strikeouts. He is one of the best young pitchers in baseball.

Nationals fans watch Stephen on the mound.

Stephen struck out Michael Bourn to start the game. He struck out two more Braves in the second inning. Stephen's teammate Ian Desmond hit a home run to give the Nationals a 1–0 lead.

Stephen struck out two batters in the third. Then he struck out two more Braves in the fourth inning and all three batters he faced in the fifth. The Nationals scored three runs to take a 4–0 lead after five innings.

Stephen allowed one run in the sixth inning. Three other pitchers finished the game for the Nationals. Washington won, 4–1. "The job isn't finished," Stephen said. "We're trying to win as many games as we can."

Stephen releases a pitch. He struck out 10 batters in the game.

The victory moved Washington closer to the playoffs. But there was talk that Stephen would be forced to end his season early. He had suffered a serious arm injury in 2010. The coaches didn't want him to throw too much and get hurt again. If the Nationals made the playoffs, would Stephen get to pitch?

Stephen heads into the clubhouse after the Nationals victory.

Stephen grew up in San Diego, California.

# CONTROLLING HIMSELF

Stephen James Strasburg was born July 20, 1988, in San Diego, California. His mother is Kathleen Swett, a **dietitian**. His father, Jim Strasburg, is a real estate developer.

Stephen loved baseball growing up. His favorite player was outfielder Tony Gwynn.

Gwynn played 20 seasons with the San Diego Padres. Stephen's favorite gift for his second birthday was a poster of Gwynn.

Tony Gwynn was selected to the Baseball Hall of Fame in 2007. The Hall of Fame is in Cooperstown, New York.

At an early age, Stephen enjoyed playing catch with his grandmother in his backyard. Stephen had a strong arm. He was big for his age. In Little League, he scared batters with his fast pitches.

Tony Gwynn fielding a ball in 1996.

In 2002, by the age of 14, Stephen could throw 90 miles per hour. But the ball didn't always go where he aimed. He also couldn't control his temper. "I had a hard time handling anything that would go wrong," Stephen said.

Stephen also had a hard time with his appetite. After practice each day at West Hills High School, he went to Estrada's Taco Shop to eat burritos and french fries. As a sophomore in 2004, he weighed 250 pounds. He was overweight. Sometimes his legs gave out. Coaches had to help him off the field. "He would just collapse," said his coach, Scott Hopgood. "It was scary. His knees couldn't support his weight." Stephen won just one game as a junior in 2005.

Stephen was an excellent student. His high school grade point average was 4.37.

Stephen learned to throw a **curveball** that fooled batters. He pitched seven complete games during his senior season. He racked up 74 strikeouts in 62.1 innings.

**Scouts** watched Stephen pitch. They thought he weighed too much. Most colleges were nervous to offer Stephen a **scholarship**. San Diego State Aztecs pitching coach Rusty Filter convinced the team's head coach, Tony Gwynn, to give Stephen a chance. Both of Stephen's parents had attended San Diego State. Stephen moved on campus. Everything seemed perfect.

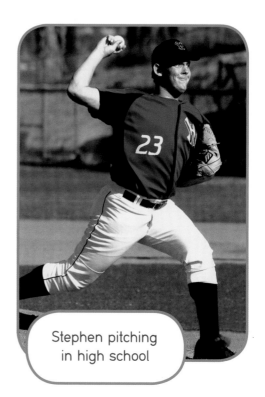

Stephen pitching in high school

Stephen *(left)* played for coach Tony Gwynn *(right)* at San Diego State University.

# WORKING HARD

Stephen was excited to play for Coach Gwynn. But things started badly. At San Diego State's first practice, the players ran 100-yard sprints. After four sprints, Stephen felt sick. He wandered into the baseball **dugout** where he threw up.

"Is there something wrong with you?" assistant coach Dave Ohton asked. Stephen was red-faced. "Just out of shape," he replied.

In the weight room, Stephen could **bench press** 115 pounds only once. He was so overweight that Coach Ohton nicknamed him Slothburg. Within a week, Stephen left school and moved back home. He was ready to quit the team. "I was going to find a job," he said.

But Stephen loved baseball too much. He returned to San Diego State. He started lifting weights and eating healthy food. Two weeks later, he passed Coach Ohton on the stairs. "I appreciate your staying on top of me," Stephen said. "Sloth," the coach replied, "you really should consider quitting. You're not going to make it." Ohton was trying to inspire Stephen with his tough words.

Stephen didn't quit. He worked harder than ever. Midway through his freshman year in 2007, his body had changed. The coaches were amazed. "After two months on campus, he went from [weighing] 255 to 225," said Gwynn. "He was killing it in the weight room. His fastball went from 91 miles an hour to 97. It happened that quick."

Stephen throws from the mound during a San Diego State game in 2009.

Stephen stood out from the beginning of his sophomore season in 2008. He struck out 23 batters against the University of Utah, despite suffering from the flu. He won eight games and was named the country's top **amateur** player by USA Baseball.

As a junior, Stephen was nearly unhittable. He had a 13–1 record and a 1.32 **earned run average (ERA)**. He also had almost twice as many strikeouts as innings pitched.

"He gets it," said Coach Gwynn. "He's very humble, and his focus is unbelievable." In his final home game as an Aztec, Stephen pitched a **no-hitter**

Stephen was the only college player selected to play for Team USA in the 2008 Olympic Games. In Beijing, China, he pitched a one-hitter against the Netherlands. He helped the United States win a bronze medal.

against the Air Force Academy. He announced he would skip his senior season to turn **pro**. He was sure to be the first player selected in the 2009 MLB **draft**.

Stephen celebrates with teammates after pitching a no-hitter in 2009.

*Sports Illustrated* called Stephen "the most-hyped pitching prospect in the history of baseball." Stephen didn't care for all the attention. "Most baseball guys love to have the fame," said Erik Castro, the Aztecs' catcher and Stephen's best friend. "But honestly, he hates it. He's more of a quiet type of kid."

Stephen is presented with his Washington Nationals jersey by teammate Ryan Zimmerman (right) in August 2009.

# NATIONAL CELEBRITY

The Washington Nationals used the first pick of the 2009 draft to select Stephen. They signed him to a four-year contract worth $15.1 million—the most ever paid to a draft choice. "Unreal!" Stephen's mother texted.

Before the season started, Stephen married Rachel Lackey in San Diego. The newlyweds traveled east to Pennsylvania where Stephen began his pro career in the **minor leagues**. He started in Class AA with the Harrisburg Senators.

ESPN broadcast Stephen's first game. He won. His first home game a few days later set an all-time attendance record for the team. Excitement swirled around him. In five starts, Stephen went 3–1 with a 1.64 ERA. "I haven't proven anything yet," he said.

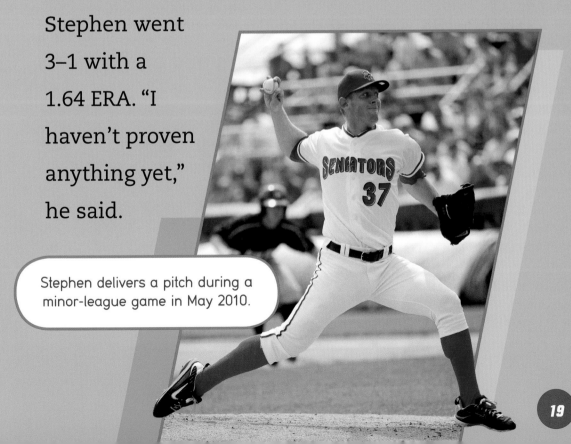

Stephen delivers a pitch during a minor-league game in May 2010.

Stephen was promoted to the Class AAA Syracuse Chiefs. His first game was played before the biggest crowd in the 135-year history of baseball in Syracuse. He pitched a one-hitter. In his second start with the Chiefs, he pitched a no-hitter. The Nationals called him up to the major leagues.

On June 8, 2010, Stephen made his MLB debut. His wife and parents were at Nationals Park, along with Coach Gwynn and others. They watched Stephen dominate the Pittsburgh Pirates. He struck out 14 batters to set a Nationals team record for strikeouts in a game. Washington won, 5–2.

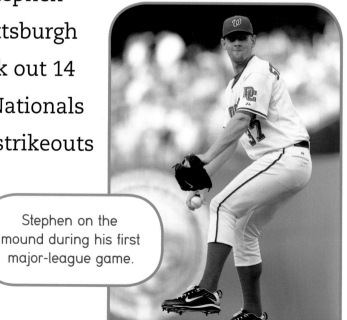

Stephen on the mound during his first major-league game.

Stephen, covered in shaving cream, shares a laugh with his father, Jim *(right)*, after Stephen's first major-league game.

"I went out there and had fun," Stephen said after the game. Teammates playfully smacked his face with three shaving cream pies. The Baseball Hall of Fame asked for Stephen's cap and a game ball.

Stephen's next game was in Cleveland. The crowd gasped when five of his first eight fastballs reached 100 miles per hour. He struck out eight batters and won again.

Stephen's third MLB game was back at Nationals Park against the Chicago White Sox. President Barack Obama and his daughters were part of the sellout crowd. They watched Stephen strike out 10 batters in seven innings. This helped set a major-league record with 32 strikeouts in a pitcher's first three starts. "That record wasn't a goal of mine," said Stephen. "My goal is to help the team win. It's all about wins and losses."

Stephen was a national celebrity. He appeared on magazine covers. He was the hot topic on radio talk shows. Stephen pretended not to notice. "Just another week," he said.

By the middle of August, Stephen had a 5–3 record and a 2.91 ERA. He had the highest strikeout rate of any pitcher in the majors. Then disaster struck. Against the Philadelphia

Phillies, Stephen threw a pitch and felt a sharp pain in his right elbow. He winced and shook his arm. The Nationals coaches and trainer raced to the mound. Stephen begged to stay in the game but was taken out. Doctors ran tests and discovered the worst. Stephen had a torn **ligament** in his elbow. Major surgery was needed. Stephen would not be able to play baseball for at least one year.

The operation doctors performed on Stephen's elbow in 2010 is called Tommy John surgery. It is named for the pitcher who first had the surgery in 1974.

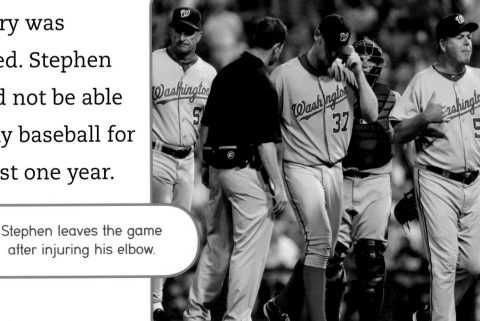

Stephen leaves the game after injuring his elbow.

Stephen wraps his arm in a towel between innings during his first MLB game after injuring his elbow.

# BETTER THAN EVER

Stephen's surgery was a success. He started a **rehabilitation** process. He stretched his arm and lifted weights. "I'm going to work as hard as I possibly can to get back out there," he said.

Stephen rebuilt his arm strength. Finally, on September 6, 2011, he returned to a major-league pitching mound. It had been more than a year since his surgery. Stephen pitched five innings against the Los Angeles Dodgers. He allowed no runs and just two hits. He pitched four more games before the season ended. He had 24 strikeouts in 24 innings with a 1.50 ERA. He was better than ever.

Stephen was excited for 2012. He hoped to play a complete season. In his first five starts, he allowed only four runs. No opponent got more than six hits against him in a game. He was named NL Pitcher of the Month for April.

Stephen throws a pitch on September 6, 2011.

Stephen pitches in 2012. The team was glad to have their ace back on the mound.

He reached 100 strikeouts faster than any other pitcher. He was voted to the **All-Star** team. "Stephen's the best pitcher in the league right now," Nationals pitching coach Steve McCatty said.

Midway through the year, Stephen learned that the Nationals were going to limit his innings. They thought he could get hurt again if he pitched too much so soon after surgery. Washington **general manager** Mike Rizzo said, "We're going to run him out there until his innings are gone and then stop him from pitching." Stephen did not like the plan. He wanted to pitch. "They're going to have to rip the ball from my hands," he said.

Stephen pitched in several more games. He had a 15–6 record. He had 197 strikeouts in 159.1 innings. But with one month left in the season, Washington shut down Stephen for the year. He had to sit and watch his teammates play. "I don't know if I'm ever going accept it, to be honest," Stephen said. "You don't grow up dreaming of playing in the big leagues to be shut down when the games start to matter."

Stephen does not care for attention from the media. But he eagerly accepted an invitation to appear on the *Late Show with David Letterman*. "He thought doing the 'Top 10' list was really cool," said a Nationals official.

Stephen's teammates and Washington fans were disappointed. The Nationals made the playoffs but lost in the first round.

The Nationals are hoping Stephen has a long career. In three brief seasons, he has shown greatness. Baseball fans everywhere talk about all the pitching records Stephen *might* break someday. Stephen doesn't understand all the fuss. He just wants to pitch. "I'm just a baseball player," Stephen says. "It's not like I'm the president or anything."

Stephen works hard but remembers to have fun.

# Selected Career Highlights

**2012**   Named to the NL All-Star team
Led NL in strikeouts into September before
his season ended

**2011**   Missed most of the season with an elbow
injury

**2010**   Set Nationals record with 14 strikeouts
in his major-league debut
Set a major-league record for
most strikeouts in his first three
games (32)
Led Major League Baseball in
strikeouts per inning ratio (13.5)
Led Class AAA Syracuse with a 1.08 ERA
Led Class AA Harrisburg with a 1.64 ERA

**2009**   Drafted with the first overall pick by the
Washington Nationals
Named First-Team All-America at
San Diego State
Set San Diego State season record with 195 strikeouts

**2008**   Helped Team USA win a bronze medal at the Olympic Games
Won Golden Spikes Award as nation's top amateur baseball player
Won Dick Case Award as USA Baseball's Athlete of the Year
Named First-Team All-America
Named Mountain West Conference Pitcher of the Year
Set San Diego State season record with 133 strikeouts
Set Mountain West Conference single-game record with 23 strikeouts
in a single game

**2007**   Only freshman to be named Second-Team All-Mountain West
Conference
Named Mountain West Conference Freshman of the Year

**2006**   Named West Hills High School Scholar Athlete of the Year
Named West Hills High School Team Most Valuable Player
Set West Hills High School season record with a 1.68 ERA

# Glossary

**ace:** in baseball, the pitcher who is the top starter on a team

**All-Star:** a player voted to play in a game held midway through the Major League Baseball season featuring the top players from the National and American leagues

**amateur:** a player who is not a professional

**Baseball Hall of Fame:** a museum where objects related to baseball's greatest players and games are displayed

**bench press:** a weight-lifting exercise done while lying on the back and pushing a barbell up from the chest

**curveball:** a slower pitch that dives as it approaches home plate

**dietitian:** a person who studies food and advises others about eating healthy

**draft:** a yearly event in which professional teams take turns choosing new players from a selected group

**dugout:** the enclosed area with a long bench along either side of a baseball field where players and coaches sit or stand during a game

**earned run average (ERA):** the number of runs a pitcher allows per nine innings. For example, if a pitcher pitches nine innings and gives up three runs, the pitcher's ERA would be 3.00.

**fastball:** a pitch that usually travels straight and very fast

**general manager:** in sports, the person who makes decisions about players, such as how much to pay each player

**ligament:** tissue in the body that connects one bone to another

**minor leagues:** a group of teams where players work to improve in hopes of moving up to the major leagues

**National League ( NL) East:** One of three divisions in the league (the West and Central are the others) comprised of the Nationals, Atlanta Braves, Philadelphia Phillies, New York Mets, and Miami Marlins

**no-hitter:** a baseball game that goes at least nine innings in which the opposing team does not get a hit

**playoffs:** a series of games held each year to decide a champion

**pro:** a player who is not an amateur and can earn money for playing

**rehabilitation:** in sports, the process of restoring a player to good health

**scholarship:** in athletics, money or other aid given to a student in exchange for playing a sport

**scouts:** people who watch and judge athletes' skills

# Further Reading & Websites

Kennedy, Mike, and Mark Stewart. *Long Ball: The Legend and Lore of the Home Run*. Minneapolis: Millbrook Press, 2006.

Savage, Jeff. *Justin Verlander*. Minneapolis: Lerner Publications Company, 2013.

Savage, Jeff. *Tim Lincecum*. Minneapolis: Lerner Publications Company, 2012.

Stewart, Mark. *The Washington Nationals*. Chicago: Norwood House Press, 2012.

The Official Site of Major League Baseball
http://www.mlb.com
Major League Baseball's official site provides fans with the latest scores and game schedules, as well as information on players, teams, and baseball history.

The Official Site of the Washington Nationals
http://washington.nationals.mlb.com
The Washington Nationals official website includes the team schedule and game results, late-breaking news, biographies of Stephen Strasburg and other players and coaches, and much more.

*Sports Illustrated Kids*
http://www.sikids.com
The *Sports Illustrated Kids* website covers all sports, including baseball.

# Index

# Photo Acknowledgments

The images in this book are used with the permission of: © Mitchell Layton/Getty Images, pp. 4, 7, 28; © Patrick McDermott/Getty Images, p. 6; AP Photo/Alex Brandon, p. 8; © Bill Cobb/SuperStock, p. 9; © Jamie Squire/Allsport/Getty Images, p. 10; Seth Poppel Yearbook Library, p. 12; AP Photo/Lenny Ignelzi, p. 13; © Donald Miralle/Getty Images, p. 15; © Peggy Peattie/U-T San Diego/ZUMA Press, p. 17; © Win McNamee/Getty Images, p. 18; © Jonathan Newton/The Washington Post via Getty Images, p. 19; © G. Fiume/Getty Images, pp. 20, 25; AP Photo/Manuel Balce Ceneta, p. 21; © Jeff Conner/Icon SMI, p. 23; AP Photo/Jacquelyn Martin, p. 24; AP Photo/Tomasso DeRosa, p. 26; © Rob Tringali/SportsChrome/Getty Images, p. 29.

Front cover: © Rob Leiter/MLB Photos via Getty Images.

Main body text set in Caecilia LT Std 55 Roman 16/28.
Typeface provided by Adobe Systems.